Weather and Storms

by Lisa Oram

PEARSON

Scott
Foresman

DK

All About Weather

Some people love rainy days. Other people prefer hot, sunny days. When we talk about rain, sun, and temperature, we are talking about **weather.** The weather affects us every day.

If you don't like the weather one day, just wait. Weather always changes. Different parts of each country usually have different kinds of weather. Everywhere you go in the world, the weather is different.

The Atmosphere

Water vapor in the atmosphere helps cause weather. The **atmosphere** is made of air that surrounds the Earth. This air is made of gases.

To understand the weather, we study the air in the atmosphere. Information about the air's moisture, speed, and temperature can tell us about the weather.

The atmosphere presses down with a force called air pressure. When the air pressure changes, the weather often changes too. Low air pressure often means the weather will be cloudy or rainy. High air pressure often makes dry, clear weather.

Scattered clouds

Thin clouds

Thunder clouds

Studying the Weather

Scientists study the weather by using special instruments. Barometers measure air pressure. Anemometers measure wind speed. Hygrometers measure water vapor in the air. The amount of water vapor in the air is called humidity. The humidity is low when air is dry and high when air is wet. They use a rain gauge while it's raining to measure how much rain has fallen.

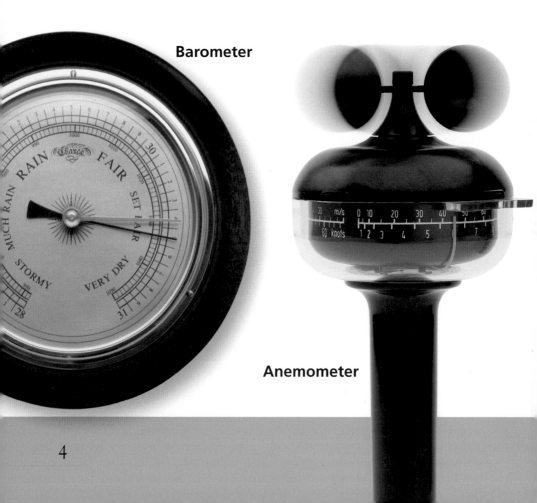

Barometer

Anemometer

Hygrometers, barometers, anemometers, and rain gauges are all important instruments. They provide information that is used to predict and record the weather.

Satellites tell what is happening with the weather. Satellites orbiting in space take pictures of the air as it moves over the Earth. Those pictures are sent back to Earth. The pictures are used to make weather maps. Weather maps show what kind of air is moving over the oceans and land. They tell us what kind of weather we'll get!

Scientists study weather maps, which use information from satellites.

Pollution and the Weather

Satellite pictures also help scientists track the pollution. Pollution can harm the Earth and change our weather.

Factories, cars, and airplanes cause pollution. They produce harmful gases. The gases get trapped in Earth's atmosphere. These gases can get heated by the Sun. This changes the gases into smog and ozone. These are forms of air pollution.

Smoke from factory chimneys harms the atmosphere.

Factories, cars, and trucks create smog. The smog pollutes the air over towns and cities. Too much smog makes it hard for people to breathe outdoors. When smog levels become harmful, weather reporters might issue a smog alert.

You can help to reduce air pollution by cutting down on car trips. You could also get rides in the cars of your friends. Using public transportation also reduces air pollution.

Cars produce gases that pollute our towns and cities.

Patterns of Weather

Weather patterns are caused by many things. The Sun, oceans, and mountains all affect weather patterns. Some places get the same weather patterns again and again. One very typical weather pattern involves snowfall in New York State. Let's take a look at how it works.

During the winter, New York State can get very cold. The air can't carry much moisture when it is cold. So why does it snow so much in New York State? New York is bordered by two of the Great Lakes, Lake Ontario and Lake Erie. The other Great Lakes are Lakes Huron, Michigan, and Superior. Lots of water evaporates from the Great Lakes, even in winter. Air moving in from the west absorbs the evaporated water. The air absorbs so much water that it can't hold it all. By the time the air is ready to release the water, it has moved east, over New York State. So the air releases the water, which falls as snow during the winter. That's why it snows so much in the areas of New York State that are closest to the Great Lakes.

Water evaporates from the Great Lakes and is carried eastward by the wind.

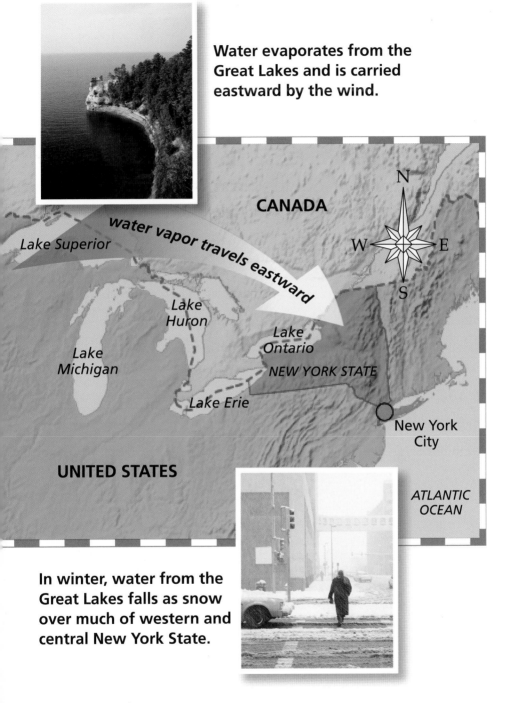

CANADA

Lake Superior

water vapor travels eastward

N
W   E
S

Lake Huron

Lake Michigan

Lake Ontario

NEW YORK STATE

Lake Erie

New York City

UNITED STATES

ATLANTIC OCEAN

In winter, water from the Great Lakes falls as snow over much of western and central New York State.

Stormy Weather

Hurricanes, tornadoes, thunderstorms, and blizzards are dangerous storms.

Hurricanes

A **hurricane** is a big storm. It forms over the warmest parts of oceans. Heat from the warm water helps cause this storm. The center of a hurricane is called the eye. Strong winds swirl around the hurricane's eye.

Hurricanes can cause a lot of damage. The heavy rain often causes flooding. Hurricane winds can blow up to 155 miles per hour. These winds can blow over buildings, power lines, and trees. If you know a hurricane is coming to your area, stay indoors.

Hurricanes are large storms that form over the ocean.

Tornadoes

A **tornado** is also
a dangerous storm. It is
different from a hurricane.
A tornado forms quickly
and moves fast over a small
area of land. Tornado winds
can reach 250 miles per hour.
Tornado winds are much
stronger than hurricane winds,
but they don't affect as large an area.

Tornadoes are sometimes called
twisters because they look like
spinning towers of air. People say
a tornado sounds like an airplane taking
off or a train roaring down its track.

Thunderstorms and Blizzards

Storms that cause rain, thunder, and lightning are called thunderstorms. Thunderstorms, which usually last for short periods of time, can also cause high winds and hail.

Hail is water that freezes inside large storm clouds. The hailstones become heavy and fall to the ground as chunks of ice.

A **blizzard** is a dangerous winter storm. During a blizzard, temperatures drop and heavy snow falls. Strong winds blow the snow into drifts. Because of the wind and the snow, it is hard to see well. People should not drive during a blizzard. It is easy to have an accident or get lost.

Snowdrifts almost buried these cabins during a blizzard.

12

Staying Safe During Storms

Storms can be dangerous. People need to know how to stay safe during them.

How do people know if a dangerous storm is coming? The National Weather Service staff monitors the weather. They send announcements to radio and TV stations. If there is a storm watch, it means a storm could happen in your area. If there is a storm warning, it means a storm is on its way. When people know that a storm is coming, they can get prepared.

The Weather and You

The seasons affect weather patterns. The weather in some seasons helps living things to grow. The weather in other seasons can hurt living things. There are many different kinds of weather, each with its own causes and effects.

Spring   **Summer**

At first you might have thought that there was little you could do about the weather. Now you know differently! By watching for National Weather Service reports, you can prepare for dangerous weather. By cutting down on car trips, you can help prevent air pollution.

Fall   **Winter**

Glossary

atmosphere   the air that surrounds the Earth

blizzard   a winter storm with low temperatures and heavy, blowing snow

hurricane   a tropical storm that forms over the ocean and causes strong winds and heavy rainfall

tornado   a spinning column of air that has high wind speeds and sometimes touches the ground

weather   what it is like outside